Ultimate Football Quiz Book

About
Premier League, World Cup
Champions League, European Championship
and more!

350
Questions
&
Answers

By Blue Heroes

Play alone or with your friends.
Test your knowledge of football.
At the end of the book, you will
find the scoreboard.
Have fun!

I will appreciate it if you leave a
review on Amazon.

Blue Heroes

1. Premier League

1. Which player scored the fastest hat-trick in the Premier League?

2. Which player, with 653 games, has made the most Premier League appearances?

3. Three players share the record for most Premier League red cards (8). Who are they?

4. With 260 goals, who is the Premier League's all-time top scorer?

5. When was the inaugural Premier League season?

6. Which team won the first Premier League title?

7. With 202 clean sheets, which goalkeeper has the best record in the Premier League?

8. How many clubs competed in the inaugural Premier League season?

9. Which three players shared the Premier League Golden Boot in 2018-19?

10. The fastest goal scored in Premier League history came in 7.69 seconds. Who scored it?

Premier League
Answers

1. Sadio Mane (2 minutes 56 seconds for Southampton vs Aston Villa in 2015)

2. Gareth Barry

3. Patrick Vieira, Richard Dunne and Duncan Ferguson

4. Alan Shearer

5. 1992-93

6. Manchester United

7. Petr Cech

8. 22

9. Pierre-Emerick Aubameyang, Mohamed Salah and Sadio Mane

10. Shane Long (for Southampton vs Watford in 2018-19)

2. World Cup

1. There have been two World Cup trophies. What was the name of the first?

2. Which country won the first ever World Cup in 1930?

3. Which country has won the most World Cups?

4. Three countries have won the World Cup twice. Can you name them?

5. Which country has appeared in three World Cup finals, but never won the competition?

6. The 2026 World Cup will be hosted across three different countries. Can you name them?

7. In which World Cup did Diego Maradona score his infamous 'Hand of God' goal?

8. The record number of World Cup goals is 16, scored by who?

9. Three people have won the World Cup as a player and as a coach. Mario Zagallo, Didier Deschamps and... can you name the third?

10. Two English players have won the World Cup Golden Boot. Who are they?

World Cup
Answers

1. Jules Rimet Trophy / Victory

2. Uruguay

3. Brazil

4. Argentina, France and Uruguay

5. Netherlands

6. United States, Canada and Mexico

7. Mexico 1986

8. Miroslav Klose

9. Franz Beckenbauer

10. Gary Lineker (1986) and Harry Kane (2018)

3. Bizarre football

1. Which Swedish footballer once had a clause inserted into his Premier League contract that prohibited him from travelling into space?

2. Which Ballon d'Or-winning footballer had a galaxy named after them in 2015?

3. Can you name the former Germany international who went on to become a professional wrestler in the WWE?

4. Which former England internationals reached number 12 in the UK Singles Chart with the 1987 song 'Diamond Lights'?

5. The England Euro '96 song 'Three Lions' was a hit by which comedy double act?

6. Which former Tottenham manager has competed in the Dakar Rally?

7. What was the name of the hotel Jose Mourinho lived in when he managed Manchester United?

8. Which Spanish club's nickname is Los Colchoneros, which translates to English as 'The Mattress Makers'?

9. English rock star Elton John was twice the owner of which football club?

10. Rangers tried to sign which superstar after Alex McLeish was alerted to his ability through popular video game Football Manager?

Bizarre football
Answers

1. Stefan Schwarz

2. Cristiano Ronaldo - Galaxy Cosmos Redshift 7 (CR7)

3. Tim Wiese

4. Chris Waddle and Glenn Hoddle (as 'Glenn and Chris')

5. David Baddiel and Frank Skinner

6. Andre Villas-Boas

7. The Lowry Hotel

8. Atletico Madrid

9. Watford

10. Lionel Messi

4. Cristiano Ronaldo & Lionel Messi

1. Messi has spent his entire professional career at Barcelona, but what was his schoolboy team?

2. Which Portuguese team did Ronaldo play for before signing for Manchester United?

3. Ronaldo is synonymous with the No.7, but what other number did he wear at Real Madrid?

4. Messi famously retired from international duty in which year before reversing his decision?

5. Ronaldo exclaims which word when celebrating a goal?

6. Messi wore the No.30 at the start of his Barca career and is now No.10. What other number has he worn for the club?

7. Which Portuguese island off the coast of Africa, which also shares its name with a cake, is Ronaldo from?

8. Messi has won a record number of Ballon d'Or awards - how many?

9. Ronaldo helped Portugal win the European Championship in which year?

10. Which German multinational sportswear company is Messi an ambassador for?

Cristiano Ronaldo & Lionel Messi

1. Newell's Old Boys

2. Sporting

3. No.9

4. 2016 (after Copa America final loss)

5. "Si!" (Spanish for 'Yes!')

6. No.19

7. Madeira

8. Six Ballon d'Or awards

9. 2016

10. Adidas

5. Champions League

1. Which club has won the most Champions League titles?

2. Who is the only player to win the Champions League with three different clubs?

3. Three people have won the Champions League a record three times as manager. Who are they?

4. In which season was the European Cup rebranded as the Champions League?

5. Which team was the first from the UK to win the European Cup?

6. The Champions League has been won only once by a team from Romania. Can you name them?

7. Liverpool have won six Champions Leagues and Manchester United have won three, but who are England's third most successful team in the competition with two titles?

8. Who is the Champions League's top goalscorer of all time?

9. Which player holds the record for most Champions League winners' medals?

10. Which outfield player appeared in the Champions League final in three different decades?

Champions League
Answers

1. Real Madrid (13)

2. Clarence Seedorf (Ajax, Real Madrid, AC Milan)

3. Bob Paisley, Carlo Ancelotti and Zinedine Zidane

4. 1992-93

5. Celtic (1966-67)

6. Steaua Bucharest (now FCSB)

7. Nottingham Forest (1978-79 and 1979-80)

8. Cristiano Ronaldo

9. Francisco Gento (six titles with Real Madrid)

10. Ryan Giggs

6. European Championship

1. In which year was the first European Championship held?

2. With three titles each, which two teams have won the most European Championships?

3. What is the name of the European Championship trophy?

4. With nine goals, who scored the most goals in a single European Championship tournament?

5. The Euro 2000 final between France and Italy was decided by Golden Goal. Which player scored the goal?

6. England's all-time leading European Championship goalscorer has a tally of seven goals. Can you name the player?

7. Which one of the following three teams has not won the European Championship: Denmark, Belgium or Greece?

8. Denmark notably won Euro 92, despite the fact that they did not initially qualify. Which team did they replace?

9. In which year did the European Championship expand from 16 teams to 24 teams?

10. Only one person has won the European Championship as a player and as manager. Can you name them?

European Championship
Answers

1. 1960

2. Germany and Spain

3. Henri Delaunay Trophy

4. Michel Platini at Euro 84

5. David Trezeguet

6. Alan Shearer

7. Belgium (runners up in 1980)

8. Yugoslavia

9. Euro 2016

10. Berti Vogts (West Germany in 1972 and

Germany in 1996)

7. True or false

1. It took Cristiano Ronaldo 27 games to score his first Champions League goal.

2. The phrase 'park the bus' arose when Jose Mourinho was forced to park the Chelsea team bus after the bus driver fell ill.

3. Singer in Irish boyband Westlife Nicky Byrne played for Leeds United before moving into music.

4. Sir Alex Ferguson managed the Scotland national team.

5. Liverpool legend Kenny Dalglish is known as 'King Kenny' because he is related to the British Royal Family.

6. Frank Lampard has scored more Premier League goals than Thierry Henry, Robbie Fowler and Michael Owen.

7. Bayern Munich star Thomas Muller is a keen chess player and once won a Bavarian chess tournament.

8. Former Brazil and Barcelona star Ronaldinho spent time in prison after being found to have used a fake passport.

9. David Beckham took ballet lessons during his time at Manchester United in order to improve his agility.

10. Brazil icon Pele once starred in a Hollywood movie alongside Michael Caine and Sylvester Stallone.

True or false
Answers

1. True

2. False

3. True

4. True

5. False

6. True

7. False

8. True

9. False

10. True

8. Bundesliga & German football

1. With 365 goals, who holds the record for top Bundesliga goalscorer of all time?

2. Bayern Munich have won the record number of Bundesliga titles, but which two clubs follow with five titles each?

3. Can you name the most capped Germany international of all time?

4. Jurgen Klopp has managed two clubs in Germany, Borussia Dortmund and - can you name the other?

5. The record age for youngest head coach in the Bundesliga is 28 years and 205 days. Who was it?

6. FC Cologne have which animal on their club crest?

7. RB Leipzig are otherwise known as...?

8. Germany have won the World Cup four times, but how many times have they done so as a unified country?

9. Only three German clubs have won the European Cup/Champions League. Can you name them?

10. What is the nickname of Borussia Monchengladbach?

Bundesliga & German football Answers

1. Gerd Muller

2. Borussia Monchengladbach and Borussia Dortmund

3. Lothar Matthaus (150 caps)

4. Mainz

5. Julian Nagelsmann (at Hoffenheim during the 2015-16 season)

6. A goat

7. The Red Bulls

8. Once (2014 - won in 1954, 1974 and 1990 as West Germany)

9. Bayern Munich, Borussia Dortmund and Hamburg

10. Die Fohlen (The Foals)

9. 'Who am I?'

1. I made my international debut for Brazil in 1993 and scored in the game. I played in two World Cup finals and my club career saw me play in Brazil, Italy, Angola, Spain, Greece and Uzbekistan.
2. I've played in Germany, Italy, Austria and France. I have won Serie A and scored the first ever Golden Goal in international football.
3. I have played in the Conference, League Two, League One, Championship, Premier League, the UEFA Cup, Champions League and the World Cup.
4. I was the first Liverpool player to win the Ballon d'Or. I scored 40 goals for my country and have played in England and Spain.
5. I was originally a striker before becoming a defender. I played 11 seasons for the same club before managing them. I've won two Bundesliga titles and a Champions League.
6. I have played for Chelsea and spent time playing in Turkey. I've been crowned African Footballer of the Year four times and the Africa Cup of Nations twice.
7. I have won league titles in Italy, Germany, Portugal and Austria. I also won the European Cup both as a player and as a manager.
8. I am the manager who first named David Beckham as England captain.
9. I've won the World Cup and European Championship at international level and I won the Champions League on two occasions as manager of two different clubs.
10. I've worn numbers 7, 17, 28 and 9 in my career, playing my football across, England, Spain, Italy and Portugal.

'Who am I?'
Answers

1. Rivaldo

2. Oliver Bierhoff

3. Steve Finnan

4. Michael Owen

5. Jurgen Klopp

6. Samuel Eto'o

7. Giovanni Trapattoni

8. Peter Taylor

9. Jupp Heynckes

10. Cristiano Ronaldo

10. Miscellaneous

1. In what league is the concept of a 'Designated Player' a feature?

2. Manchester United famously wear red, but what colours did they wear before adopting red?

3. Which club is associated with 'Galacticos'?

4. Which manager was famously said to have given players 'the Hairdryer Treatment'?

5. Which club is sometimes referred to as FC Hollywood?

6. In English football what is 'St Totteringham's Day'?

7. After Juventus, AC Milan and Inter, with nine Scudettos, which team has won the most Serie A titles?

8. In Spanish football, what is 'the Pichichi'?

9. In video game FIFA 20, team Piemonte Calcio represents which real-life club?

10. Which MLS franchise team does David Beckham own?

Miscellaneous
Answers

1. Major League Soccer (MLS)

2. Green and gold

3. Real Madrid

4. Sir Alex Ferguson

5. Bayern Munich

6. The date on which it is mathematically impossible for Tottenham to finish above Arsenal

7. Genoa

8. The award given to the top goalscorer (named after Rafael "Pichichi" Moreno).

9. Juventus

10. Inter Miami

11. Premier League part 2

1. Which Premier League winner's father played rugby for Wales?

2. What year did the Premier League start?

3. Who was the first sponsor of the Premier League?

4. In what season did Roman Abramovich take over Chelsea?

5. Which player holds the record for the most goals in consecutive Premier League games?

6. Kevin Phillips won the Golden Boot in 1999/2000, who was the next English player to do so?

7. Which player holds the record for most consecutive Premier League appearances (310)?

8. What was significant about Mario Balotelli's only assist in the Premier League for Manchester City?

9. Who scored the first 'perfect hat-trick' (left foot, right foot, and header) in the Premier League?

10. What player scored four goals in 12 minutes after coming on as a sub versus Nottingham Forest?

Premier League part 2
Answers

1. Ryan Giggs

2. 1992

3. Carling

4. 2003/04

5. Jamie Vardy

6. Harry Kane

7. Brad Friedel

8. It was for Sergio Aguero's title-winning goal vs QPR

9. Jimmy Floyd Hasselbaink

10. Ole Gunnar Solskjaer

12. Premier League part 3

1. Which goalkeeper has the record of 138 clean sheets for the same Premier League team?

2. How many clubs have never been relegated from the Premier League?

3. How many teams were in the first ever Premier League?

4. The lowest attendance was 3,039 in 1993 when Everton played away to which club?

5. Which two non-English clubs have played in the Premier League?

6. How many times has the league been renamed?

7. Which Swede had a clause in his contract banning him from traveling into space?

8. In 2005, Newcastle's Lee Bowyer had an on-pitch scrap with which team-mate?

9. For what club did Paulo Di Canio play when he pushed referee Paul Alcock?

10. Against which team did Wayne Rooney score his Premier League first goal?

Premier League part 3
Answers

1. Petr Cech

2. Six

3. 22

4. Wimbledon

5. Swansea City and Cardiff City

6. Four

7. Stefan Schwarz

8. Kieron Dyer

9. Sheffield Wednesday

10. Arsenal

13. Premier League part 4 - Managers

1. Who was the first Premier League manager to be sacked?

2. Who was Jose Mourinho's first signing at Chelsea?

3. How many times had David Moyes won the prestigious LMA Manager of the year award?

4. Who was the first Italian manager to win the Premier League?

5. Which manager was in charge at Manchester City when they won their first Premier League title?

6. Who has managed Reading, Swansea and Liverpool?

7. Which club did Glenn Hoddle join after being sacked as England manager in 1999?

8. How many times did Sir Alex Ferguson win the Premier League Manager of the Month award?

9. Who was the first English manager to win Premier League Manager of the Year award?

10. Ron Atkinson last managed which club in the Premier League?

Premier League part 4 – Managers Answers

1. Ian Porterfield

2. Paulo Ferreira

3. Three

4. Carlo Ancelotti

5. Roberto Mancini

6. Brendan Rodgers

7. Southampton

8. Twenty-seven (27)

9. Harry Redknapp

10. Nottingham Forest

14. Premier League part 5 – Goals

1. Who scored the first ever Premier League goal?

2. Which England player scored in 46 different Premier League games throughout his career?

3. Who is the only person born before 1960 to score a Premier League hat-trick?

4. Who is the Premier League's all-time leading goal scorer?

5. Which team lost two games by an eight-goal margin in 2009-2010?

6. Which player holds the record for scoring the most goals in his debut Premier League season?

7. The highest scoring Premier League game finished 7-4. Which two teams played?

8. Who scored the first Premier League hat-trick?

9. Name the player that scored the fastest Premier League hat-trick?

10. Who was the first ever winner of the Premier League's Golden Boot?

Premier League part 5 – Goals
Answers

1. Brian Deane

2. Darius Vassell

3. Gordon Strachan

4. Alan Shearer

5. Wigan Athletic

6. Kevin Phillips

7. Portsmouth and Reading

8. Eric Cantona

9. Sadio Mane

10. Teddy Sheringham

15. Premier League part 6 – Champions and Relegation

1. Who went down in 1996-97 after being deducted three points?

2. Which striker made the PFA Team of the Year in 2004-05 despite being relegated?

3. Which team embarrassingly recorded the fewest points ever in a Premier League season?

4. Who was the first outfield player to play every minute of the season for a Premier League title-winning side?

5. In what season did Arsenal's 'Invincibles' go the whole season unbeaten?

6. Who won the first Premier League title?

7. Which club conceded 100 goals on the way to being relegated in 1993/94?

8. Which club were relegated in their first season in the Premier League in 1997/98?

9. Who are the only team to have received a gold version of the Premier League trophy?

10. How many times did Alex Ferguson win the Premier League?

Premier League part 6 – Champions and Relegation
Answers

1. Middlesbrough

2. Andy Johnson

3. Derby County

4. Gary Pallister

5. 2003/04

6. Manchester United

7. Swindon Town

8. Barnsley

9. Arsenal

10. Thirteen (13)

16. European Football

1. The winners of the UEFA Champions League and the UEFA Europe League compete for which sporting trophy?

2. Which variant of the game of football has its own UEFA Championship?

3. "La Liga" is the name of which European country's professional football association?

4. The professional football association of which European country is called "Serie A"?

5. Name the Dutch footballer who was voted "European Player of the Century" in 1999.

6. Which French player is a record-scoring footballer for Arsenal and went on to become Assistant Manager of Belgium?

7. Which player went through the Ajax youth system, played for Ajax and became Assistant Manager at the club in 2011?

8. Name the Juventus goalkeeper who was the first winner of the Golden Foot Award.

9. Who started their professional football career at Stuttgarter Kickers, became captain of the German team and then head coach of the USA team?

10. How much did Sporting Lisbon receive for the transfer of 17 years old, Cristiano Ronaldo?

European Football
Answers

1. UEFA Super Cup

2. Futsal

3. Spain

4. Italy

5. Johan Cruyff

6. Thierry Henry

7. Denis Bergkamp

8. Gianluigi Buffon

9. Jurgen Klinsmann

10. £12 million, a record fee at the time for a player of his age.

17. European Football – Stadiums

Guess the football club.

1. Camp Nou

2. Signal Iduna Park (Wesfalenstadion)

3. San Siro (Stadio Giuseppe Meazza)

4. Parc de Princes

5. Turk Telekom Stadium

6. Santiago Bernabeu

7. Estadio da Luz

8. Amsterdam Arena

9. Mestalla

10. Allianz Arena

European Football – Stadiums Answers

1. Barcelona

2. Borussia Dortmund

3. AC Miland and Inter

4. Paris Saint-Germain

5. Galatasaray

6. Real Madrid

7. Benfica Lisbon

8. Ajax

9. Valencia

10. Bayern Munich

18. World Cup

1. In the 2010 World Cup final, referee Howard Webb handed out nine yellow cards to Dutch players; who got two and was sent off?

2. Who scored the goal that enabled the Republic of Ireland to beat Italy at the 1994 World Cup finals?

3. Which player scored a goal for Italy in the World Cup finals and also played in the Premier League?

4. Name the player that, aged forty, was the oldest World Cup winning captain?

5. Which three members of the England World Cup squad from 2010 were traveling to their third World Cup tournament?

6. Scotland had appeared eight times at the World Cup finals; how many times have they made it past the group stage?

7. Who is the highest scorer in World Cup finals for the Netherlands, with seven goals?

8. Who scored the winning goal against Tunisia in the group stages of WC 2018?

9. Which player won the World Cup Young Player award in 2018?

10. Harry Kane was the top scorer of the World Cup 2018. Who came second?

World Cup
Answers

1. Johnny Heitinga

2. Ray Houghton

3. Dino Baggio

4. Dino Zoff (Italy, 1982)

5. David James, Ashley Cole and Joe Cole

6. None

7. Johnny Rep

8. Harry Kane (scored both goals)

9. Kylian Mbappe

10. Antoine Griezmann and Romelu Lukaku – both with 4 goals

19. Champions League

1. Which were the first two teams from the same European football league to contest a European or Champions League final?

2. Who was the first Brit to win the Champions League?

3. Who were the first team to win the Champions League the year after winning the UEFA Cup/ Europa League?

4. What links Marcel Desailly, Paolo Sousa, Gerard Pique, and Samuel Eto'o?

5. Which were the first three teams to win the Champions League without ever having won the European Cup?

6. Which player had 13 years between his two Champions League wins, in 1995 and 2008?

7. Which legendary Hungarian won three European Cups with Real Madrid in 1959, 1960 and 1966?

8. What links Real Madrid (in 1966), Celtic (in 1967) and Steaua Bucharest (in 1986)?

9. Who was the first player to win the Champions League with three different clubs?

10. Who were the first team to have won the tournament without being champions of their domestic league?

Champions League
Answers

1. Real Madrid and Valencia, in 2000

2. Paul Lambert with Borussia Dortmund, in 1997

3. Porto (2002/03 and then 2003/04)

4. They won successive Champions Leagues with different teams: Desailly (Marseilles and AC Milan), Sousa (Juventus and Dortmund), Pique (Man Utd and Barcelona), Eto'o (Barcelona and Inter Milan)

5. Marseille, Borussia Dortmund and Chelsea

6. Edwin van der Sar, with Juventus and then Manchester United

7. Ferenc Puskás

8. They all won the European Cup fielding only local players.

9. Clarence Seedorf, with Ajax in 1995, Real Madrid in 1998, and with AC Milan in 2003 and 2007

10. Nottingham Forest. Forest won the English League in 1978 before winning the European Cup in 1979 and defending it in 1980. They did not win the English League in 1979

20. Winners & Finalists of The Champions League

1. Who were the first team to win the European Cup, in 1956?

2. Who were the first Italian team to win the European Cup?

3. Having won back to back titles in the 1960s, which team lost the next five finals in which they played?

4. Which club was Champions League runner up five times in the first twenty-five years of the competition?

5. Which was the first English men's team to win the European Cup?

6. Which was the first English women's team to win the Champions League?

7. Which was the first English team to win the European Cup/Champions League twice?

8. As of 2020, which country had the greatest number of different winners?

9. Which was the first team from Eastern Europe to win the European Cup?

10. Never European Cup winners, which were the first Italian team to reach the final?

Winners & Finalists of The Champions League
Answers

1. Real Madrid. They won it the first five years.

2. AC Milan

3. Benfica (1963, 1965, 1968, 1988 and 1990)

4. Juventus

5. Manchester United, at Wembley in 1968.

6. Arsenal

7. Liverpool, in 1977 and 1978

8. England, with five

9. Steaua Bucharest

10. Fiorentina

21. Captains of European CUP and Champions League

1. Who was the first player to captain their team to three victories in the top European trophy?

2. Ajax won the European cup three years in a row in the early seventies, with three different captains. Name any of them…

3. Which goalkeeper captained Barcelona to their European Cup, at Wembley in 1992?

4. Who was the first captain to score in a Champions League final? (Not including a penalty shoot out, though the goal was a penalty, but in normal time).

5. Who captained Manchester United to their first European Cup victory?

6. Nicknamed 'El Tractor', who lead Inter to their 2010 victory?

7. Which future Question of Sport captain wore the armband for Liverpool's first two European Cup victories?

8. Who was the first Champions League (as opposed to European Cup) winning Captain?

9. Who are the first father-son combination to both captain their team to European Cup/ Champions League victory?

10. Roy Keane, Manchester United's captain for the 1998/99 season, was suspended for the Champions League final. Who wore the armband for the Premier League team in his place?

Captains of European CUP and Champions League
Answers

1. Franz Beckenbauer. Bayern Munich won it in 1974, 1975 and 1976

2. Velibor Vasović, Piet Keizer or Johan Cruyff

3. Andoni Zubizarreta

4. Steffan Effenberg

5. Bobby Charlton, in 1968

6. Javier Zanetti

7. Emlyn Hughes

8. Didier Deschamps, aged only 24

9. Cesare Maldini (AC Milan, 1963) and Paolo Maldini (AC Milan, 2007)

10. Peter Schmeichel, in his last game for the club

22. Champions League Goal Scorers

1. Which Ivorian has 41 Champions League goals, including five for Marseille and five for Galatasaray?

2. Which Dutchman has 29 Champions League goals, scored for Deportivo de La Coruña and Bayern Munich (including one after just 10.12 seconds)?

3. Who scored 34 goals in 35 European Cup games?

4. Which Brazilian scored 30 Champions League goals – 25 for AC Milan and five for Real Madrid?

5. Who scored 25 Champions League goals for Parma, Lazio, Inter Milan, Chelsea and AC Milan?

6. Who made 89 Champions League appearances for Juventus, scoring 42 goals?

7. Who scored 46 goals in 81 games for Juventus and AC Milan?

8. Which player has scored 21 goals in 60 Champions League games for Bayern, Atlético Madrid and Juventus?

9. Who scored 35 European Cup goals in 41 games for Honvéd and Real Madrid?

10. Who scored 56 Champions League goals (excluding qualification games), eight of which were for PSV?

Champions League Goal Scorers
Answers

1. Didier Drogba

2. Roy Makaay

3. Gerd Müller

4. Kaká

5. Hernan Crespo

6. Alesandro del Piero

7. Filippo Inzaghi

8. Mario Mandžukić

9. Ferenc Puskás

10. Ruud van Nistelrooy

23. First Player From Their Country To Win The UEFA Champions League

1. Which Serbian was the first from his country to win the Champions League, in 2008?

2. Who was the first Egyptian to win the Champions League?

3. Who was the first Costa Rican to win the Champions League?

4. Who, in 2010, became the first Colombian to win the Champions League?

5. Zvonomir Boban was the second Croat to win the Champions League. Which striker was the first?

6. Who was the first Finn to win the Champions League?

7. Which two players were the first Czechs to win the Champions League, one scoring a goal from open play and also in a penalty shoot out?

8. Who was the first Ghanaian to win the Champions League?

9. Two Nigerians won the Champions League in the same year in the mid 90's. Who were they?

10. Who was the first player from the Ivory Coast to win the Champions League?

First Player From Their Country To Win The UEFA Champions League Answers

1. Nemanja Vidić of Manchester United

2. Mohamed Salah, with Liverpool in 2019

3. Keylor Navas, with Real Madrid in 2016

4. Iván Córdoba

5. Alen Bokšić. He scored six goals in that season's competition

6. Jari Litmanen

7. Milan Baroš and Vladimír Šmicer

8. Marseille's Abédi Pelé in 1993

9. Finidi George and Nawankwo Kanu, for Ajax in 1995

10. Yaya Toure, with Barcelona in 2009

24. Champions League Goal Scorers & Assist Makers

1. Who was the was the first man to score for six different clubs in the Champions League, including five teams who had previously won the tournament, but never won the competition himself?

2. Who scored four goals against Real Madrid in the first leg of the 2012/2013 semi-final?

3. Which Liverpool player set a new record for the number of assists in a campaign during the 2018 Champions League final?

4. Which Dortmund player chipped Angelo Peruzzi within 16 seconds of coming on as a substitute in a final?

5. Who was the first player to score in two Champions League final matches for the winning team?

6. Which Brazilian scored the winning goal for Barcelona against Arsenal in 2006?

7. On "that night in Barcelona" who scored a free kick for Bayern Munch?

8. Who scored two first half goals for AC Milan in the 2005 final?

9. Who were the first two Englishmen to score in a Champions League Final?

10. In the 2019 final, whose pass hit Moussa Sissoko's arm to earn his team a penalty?

Champions League Goal Scorers & Assist Makers
Answers

1. Zlatan Ibrahimović – The teams he scored for in the Champions League who had previously won it are Ajax, Barcelona, Milan and Juventus. Inter would win it the season after he left. He also scored for PSG. He never played for Manchester United in the Champions League. His first club, Malmö, were European Cup runners up in 1978/79

2. Robert Lewandowski

3. James Milner

4. Lars Ricken

5. Raúl. He won the competition in 1998, 2000 and 2002, scoring in the latter two of those

6. Juliano Belletti

7. Mario Basler

8. Hernan Crespo

9. Teddy Sheringham, in 1999 (for Manchester United), and Steve McManaman in 2000 (for Real Madrid)

10. Sadio Mane's. Though it may well be that he was aiming for the naively outstretched arm

25. Champions League Managers

1. Who managed both Borussia Dortmund and Bayern Munich to Champions League titles?

2. Who famously did a knee-slide after Maniche scored at Old Trafford?

3. Three Argentinians were the first three managers from outside of Europe to reach a Champions League final. Name them.

4. Which manager set a record of 190 Champions League games managed?

5. Who won the European Cup / Champions League as a player twice with one team, once with another (as an elder statesman in a young team), and once more as a manager with a third?

6. Which nomadic coach won 'La Decima'?

7. Which manager won the UEFA Cup (with a Spanish team) and the Champions League (with an English team) in consecutive seasons?

8. Which Romanian manager has managed Inter Milan (3 times), Galatasaray (26), Beşiktaş (6), Shakhtar Donetsk (68) between 1998 and 2016? He also won the UEFA Cup with Shaktar in 2009.

9. Which manager set a record for being the youngest coach to manage in a Champions League match with Hoffenheim (31 years, 58 days) and to win a Champions League match with RB Leipzig (32 years, 56 days).

10. Who was the first manager win the Champions League, the World Cup and the European Championship?

Champions League Managers Answers

1. Ottmar Hitzfeld
2. Jose Mourinho
3. Héctor Cúper (2000 & 2001 with Valencia), Diego Simeone (2014 & 2016 with Atlético Madrid) and Mauricio Pochettino (2019 with Tottenham Hotspur)
4. Sir Alex Ferguson
5. Frank Rijkaard, who won it twice with Milan (1989 and 1990), with Ajax (in 1995) and with Barcelona (in 2006)
6. Carlo Ancelotti managed Real Madrid to their tenth title. Teams he has managed include Parma, Juventus, Milan, Chelsea, PSG, Real Madrid, Bayern Munich, and Napoli
7. Rafael Benitez (won the UEFA Cup in 2004 with Valencia and the Champions League in 2005 with Liverpool)
8. Mircea Lucescu. Lucescu can speak seven languages: English, Portuguese, Spanish, Italian, French and Russian as well as his native Romanian
9. Julian Nagelsmann
10. Vicente del Bosque on the Champions League with Real Madrid in 2000 and 2002, the World Cup in 2010 and the European Championship in 2012 with Spain

26. Champions League Stadiums

1. Which club played at the Arnold Schwarzenegger Stadium?

2. Which stadium was the venue for Liverpool's 1977 and 1984 triumphs?

3. What links Real Madrid in 1957, Inter Milan in 1965, Manchester United in 1968, Ajax in 1972, Liverpool in 1978 and Borussia Dortmund in 1997?

4. In November 2019, the TripAdvisor reviews of the stadiums of that season's clubs were ranked. Which came top?

5. Who were the first English team to lose a European Cup/ Champions League final in England?

6. A study was done looking at games played behind closed doors in the Champions League between 2002/03 and 2019. In normal matches, the home team won 49.3% of the time. For matches behind closed doors, what was the most likely outcome: a home win, a draw or an away win?

7. Which was the first country to hold a Champions League final that had not, to that point, had one of its clubs reach even the group stage of the competition?

8. The UEFA Champions League anthem is played at the stadium before every game. Written by Tony Britten, it is an adaptation of which piece of Handel's music?

9. At what ground did Real Madrid famously beat Eintracht Frankfurt 7-3 in 1960?

10. The 1985 European Cup final between Juventus and Liverpool was held at which stadium?

Champions League Stadiums
Answers

1. Sturm Graz
2. The Olympic Stadium in Rome
3. They all won the European Cup or Champions League on home soil. Real Madrid 2-0 Fiorentina (1957, Madrid), Inter Milan 1-0 Benfica (1965, Milan), Manchester United 4-1 Benfica (1968, Wembley), Ajax 2-0 Inter Milan (1972, Rotterdam), Liverpool 1-0 Club Brugge (1978, Wembley) and Borussia Dortmund 3-1 Juventus (1997, Munich)
4. Liverpool's Anfield stadium was first, with an average of 4.5 stars. Dortmund's stadium was second and Juventus's third
5. Manchester United, beaten by Barcelona at Wembley in 2011. They were also the first English team to win a European Cup in England, at Wembley in 1968
6. An away win – 42.1% of games ended with this result. (Echoes: what happens when football is played behind closed doors? Reade, Schreyer & Singleton, 2020)
7. Wales. Real Madrid beat Juventus 4-1 at the Millennium Stadium in 2017
8. Zadok the Priest
9. Hampden Park
10. Heysel Stadium, Brussels, Belgium

27. Who am I? Champions League

1. I set a record for Champions League appearances with 177, for Real Madrid and Porto. Who am I?

2. I set the record number of Champions League appearances for a single club, with 151. Who am I?

3. I have been sent off for all of Arsenal, Juventus and Inter Milan in the Champions League. Who am I?

4. I am the club who set a record for ten consecutive clean sheets, ending with Samuel Eto'o scoring in the 76th minute of a game on 17 May 2006. Which club am I?

5. I have 107 appearances between 1994-2013 with Manchester United, Real Madrid, Milan and PSG. Who am I?

6. I am the club, who incidentally had never won their domestic league, which lost to Real Madrid in the final having beaten Liverpool and Manchester United in the quarter and semi-finals. Which club am I?

7. I was European Cup top scorer in 1988/89 and the European Championship top scorer in 1988. Who am I?

8. I set a record as the youngest captain in the Champions League, leading Porto against Maccabi Tel Aviv in 2015–16, aged 18 years and 221 days. Who am I?

9. I became the first player to reach the Champions League quarter-finals with four separate clubs: Kaiserslautern, Bayer Leverkusen, Bayern and Chelsea. Munich and Chelsea. Who am I?

10. I am a specialist set piece taking defender who was joint top scorer in the 1993/94 competition. I also scored in a previous European Cup final. Who am I?

Who am I? Champions League Answers

1. Iker Casillas, with 150 for Real and 27 for Porto

2. Xavi, of Barcelona

3. Patrick Vieira

4. Arsenal. After not conceding for 995 minutes, Samuel Eto'o scored against them in the final

5. David Beckham

6. Bayer Leverkusen lost to Real Madrid in the 2002 final

7. Marco van Basten

8. Ruben Neves

9. Michael Ballack

10. Ronald Koeman

28. Difficult Champions League

1. Who was the referee for the 1999 final?

2. Which was the first team to ever knock Real Madrid out of the European Cup?

3. Which goalkeeper was the first player to win European Cup winners' medals with two different English clubs?

4. What links Andriy Shevchenko, Vladimir Jugovic, Didier Drogba and Cristiano Ronaldo?

5. Name the three future Bolton players to feature for Real Madrid in the 2000 final.

6. When Jens Lehmen was sent off in the 2006 final, who came on for Robert Pires as a replacement for him in goal?

7. The 1962 European Cup final pitted the clubs that won the two previous tournaments. Which clubs?

8. Two weeks prior to the all German Champions League final in 2013, which Dortmund player announced he would be going Bayern at the end of the season?

9. Who is the first player to win the Champions League with two different British clubs?

10. What do Ferenc Puskás, Zoltán Czibor, Gerd Muller, Mario Mandžukić and Zinedine Zidane have in common?

Difficult Champions League Answers

1. Pierluigi Collina

2. Barcelona

3. Jimmy Rimmer, with Manchester United in 1968 (as an unused substitute) and Aston Villa in 1982

4. They have all scored the conclusive penalty in Champions League penalty shoot outs

5. Ivan Campo, Nicolas Anelka and Fernando Hierro

6. Manuel Almunia

7. Benfica (who beat Barcelona in 1961) and Real Madrid (who famously beat Eintracht Frankfurt 7-3 in 1960). Benfica won 5-3

8. Mario Götze. He got eight assists in that Champions League campaign but was injured for the match

9. Daniel Sturridge, with Chelsea and Liverpool – he was an unused substitute in the 2012 and 2019 finals

10. They all scored in a European Cup / Champions League final and in a World Cup final

29. FIFA World Cup

1. Which was the first FIFA World Cup Finals tournament to feature substitutes?

2. How many FIFA World Cup Finals have Australia qualified for?

3. Which host Nation of the FIFA Women's World Cup Finals was the only one to win the competition?

4. Who scored England's goal against Ireland in the 1990 World Cup Finals in Italy?

5. Who were the first Asian team to qualify for a FIFA World Cup Finals tournament?

6. Which 1970 FIFA World Cup Finals England squad player had yet to win a full cap?

7. Which four USA players scored at the 2014 FIFA World Cup Finals?

8. Who were the Top Five Goalscorers at the 1970 FIFA World Cup Finals in Mexico?

9. Which five players affiliated to AC Milan participated in the 2018 FIFA World Cup Finals in Russia?

10. Which FIFA World Cup Golden Boot Winner saw his Nation eliminated after the Group Stage Phase?

FIFA World Cup

Answers

1. The first FIFA World Cup Finals tournament to feature substitutes was Mexico 1970: Anatoly Puzach of the USSR was the first used substitute in the opening game against Mexico.

2. Australia qualified for Four FIFA World Cup Finals: 1974 West Germany, 2006 Germany, 2010 South Africa and 2014 Brazil.

3. The United States of America in 1999 is the only host Nation of the FIFA Women's World Cup Finals to win the competition.

4. Gary Lineker scored England's goal against Ireland in the 1990 World Cup Finals in Italy in the Group F match finished 1-1 with Kevin Sheedy scoring for the Republic of Ireland.

5. The Dutch East Indies (now Indonesia) at the 1938 World Cup in France.

6. Leeds United's striker Alan 'Sniffer' Clarke had yet to win a full England Cap before the 1970 FIFA World Cup Finals in Mexico began.

7. Clint Dempsey (2 goals), Julian Green, John Brooks and Jermaine Jones.

8. The Top Five Goalscorers at the 1970 FIFA World Cup Finals in Mexico were Gerd Müller (West Germany, 10 goals), Jairzinho (Brazil, 7 goals), Teófilo Cubillas (Peru, 5 goals), Pelé (Brazil, 4 goals) and Anatoliy Byshovets (Soviet Union, 4 goals).

9. The five players affiliated to AC Milan who participated in the 2018 FIFA World Cup Finals in Russia Lucas Biglia (Argentina), André Silva (Portugal), Nikola Kalinić (Croatia), Cristián Zapata (Colombia) and Ricardo Rodríguez (Switzerland).

10. Oleg Salenko of Russia is the only player ever to win the World Cup Golden Boot award with a team eliminated from the FIFA World Cup Finals at the group stage at the 1994 Finals in the United States.

30. La Liga

1. In what year was La Liga formed?

2. Who has more La Liga titles - Real Madrid or Barcelona?

3. How many teams make up La Liga?

4. Which three clubs were promoted to La Liga for the 2019/20 season?

5. Who has made the most La Liga appearances?

6. Which company is the current main sponsor of La Liga?

7. How many combined La Liga titles have Real Madrid and Barcelona won?

8. Which club is La Liga's third most successful team?

9. Which is the only club, other than Real Madrid and Barcelona, never to have played outside the Spanish top division?

10. Who is the only African footballer to win the La Liga Golden Boot?

La Liga
Answers

1. 1929

2. Real Madrid

3. 20

4. Osasuna, Granada and Mallorca

5. Andoni Zubizarreta

6. Santander

7. 59

8. Atletico Madrid

9. Athletic Bilbao

10. Samuel Eto'o

31. Mixed

1. Who was the last Manchester United player to win the Ballon d'Or before Cristiano Ronaldo?

2. Which current Premier League team has launched a bid to be officially recognised as the oldest professional club in the world?

3. Which player has made the most appearances in Premier League history?

4. Which team has spent the most seasons in Serie A? (88)

5. Which Sheffield United striker scored the first goal ever in the Premier League in 1992/93?

6. Name the top two teams in the English Championship prior to lockdown.

7. How many top division domestic titles had Chelsea won prior to their first triumph of the Roman Abramovich era in 2004/05?

8. Which former Premier League team was sponsored by TY – owners of the Beanie Babies franchise – between 2002 and 2005?

9. Alan Shearer is the all-time top Premier League goalscorer – how many did he score?

10. Which goalkeeper kept the most clean sheets in Premier League history?

Mixed
Answers

1. George Best

2. Crystal Palace

3. Gareth Barry (632)

4. Inter

5. Brian Deane

6. Leeds, West Brom

7. One

8. Portsmouth

9. 260

10. Petr Cech (202)

32. Mixed part II

1. One side in 2018/19 became the first team to not draw a single game away from home in the Premier League. Name the team.

2. Has Zlatan Ibrahimovic won the Champions League in his career?

3. What is so significant about Mario Balotelli's only assist for Manchester City in the Premier League?

4. Which team plays their football at Estadio da Luz?

5. With 170 caps to her name, which player has made the most appearances for the England women's national team?

6. Brazil have won the World Cup more times than any other team with five triumphs. Which two nations are joint-second with four World Cup titles?

7. Which British team has won the European Cup more times than its own domestic top league?

8. Fans of Dutch side ADO Den Haag stormed the club's training ground in February 2020 to confront their manager – a British former Premier League boss – over his poor tactics. Name the manager.

9. Name the only ever English winner of the European Golden Boot.

10. How many West Ham players were named in the England starting XI for the 1966 World Cup final?

Mixed part II
Answers

1. Tottenham

2. No

3. Set up Sergio Aguero to win the Premier League v QPR

4. Benfica

5. Fara Williams

6. Italy and Germany

7. Nottingham Forest

8. Alan Pardew

9. Kevin Phillips (Sunderland – 30 goals in 1999/2000)

10. Three (Bobby Moore, Martin Peters, Geoff Hurst)

33. Mixed part III

1. Who is the only player to win the Champions League with three different clubs?

2. Which player was sold for the highest transfer fee ever received by a Premier League team?

3. Who is Manchester City's record signing?

4. In 1986, defender Alvin Martin scored a hat-trick in an 8-1 victory over Newcastle. What was so peculiar about his achievement?

5. How many Ballon d'Or awards has Lionel Messi won?

6. Which Premier League or EFL team is known as: The Chairboys

7. Which Premier League or EFL team is known as: The Cod Army

8. Which Premier League or EFL team is known as: The Hornets

9. Which Premier League or EFL team is known as: The Railwaymen

10. Which Premier League or EFL team is known as: The Valiants

Mixed part III
Answers

1. Clarence Seedorf (Ajax, Real Madrid, AC Milan)

2. Philippe Coutinho (£105m – Liverpool to Barcelona)

3. Rodri

4. He scored against three different goalkeepers

5. Six

6. Wycombe Wanderers

7. Fleetwood Town

8. Watford

9. Crewe Alexandra

10. Port Vale

34. Mixed part IV

1. As of December 2018, name the four football managers to manage in the Premier League at the age of over 70?

2. Which two clubs play in the M23 derby?

3. In the 2018/19 Premier League, starting with the lowest, which three clubs had the smallest stadium capacities?

4. Which British team defeated Barcelona both home and away in a 1966/67 European Cup competition and also reached the semi-final of the 1984 European Cup?

5. Who once said: "Football is a simple game. Twenty-two men chase a ball for 90 minutes and at the end, the Germans always win."?

6. If it was Naranjito in 1982, and Juanito in 1970, what was it in 1966?

7. Billy Wright, the first footballer in the world to earn 100 international caps, spent his whole career at which football club?

8. Three teams have sat at the top of the Premier League only to be relegated in the same season; can you name them?

9. Name the top Premier League goalscorer to never have been capped for his country? (Hint: he now has a son named Tyrese playing for Stoke City)

10. Four Manchester United players have won the European Footballer of the Year award; can you name them?

Mixed part IV
Answers

1. Sir Alex Ferguson, Sir Bobby Robson, Roy Hodgson and Neil Warnock

2. Brighton and Crystal Palace

3. Bournemouth (Vitalty Stadium -11,464), Burnley (Turf Moor - 21,401) and Watford (Vicarage Road - 23,700)

4. Dundee United

5. Gary Lineker

6. World Cup Willie (World Cup host mascots)

7. Wolverhampton Wanderers

8. Charlton (1998/99), Bolton (2011/12), and Hull City (2016/17)

9. Kevin Campbell

10. Denis Law (1964), Bobby Charlton (1966), George Best (1968), and Cristiano Ronaldo (2008)

35. Mixed part V

1. What was introduced for the first time by trainer Donald Colman in the 1920s at Pittodrie Stadium, Aberdeen?

2. As of 2017, which European football club has supplied a player in the starting line-up of every World Cup final since 1982?

3. What's different about the recently launched limited edition Subbuteo table football set featuring Arsenal and Chelsea teams?

4. England first entered the Football World Cup in 1950; how many tournaments have they failed to qualify for since then?

5. Name the football club with which Jose Mourinho first became a top-tier manager?

6. Jamie Carragher made his first team debut for Liverpool under which manager?

7. Ryan Giggs is the new Wales football manager, but in which sport was his father Danny Wilson a Welsh international?

8. Which Russian footballer, nicknamed the "Black Panther", is widely regarded as the greatest goalkeeper in the history of the sport?

9. Which adhesive manufacturer sponsors two English association football leagues at levels 7–8 of the English football league system?

10. Can you name the only footballer born before 1960 to score a Premier League hat-trick (Hint: The Premier League was founded in 1992)?

Mixed part V
Answers

1. Dugouts (also, in 1978, Pittodrie became the second all-seated stadium in Great Britain)

2. Bayern Munich

3. The figures are female

4. Three (1974 (West Germany), 1978 (Argentina) and 1994 (United States))

5. Benfica

6. Roy Evans (in 1997)

7. Rugby League

8. Lev Yashin

9. Evo-Stik

10. Gordon Strachan

Scores

No.	N	S	N	S	N	S	N	S	W

No. - questions name
number

N - player name

S - score

w - who won

Scores

No.	N	S	N	S	N	S	N	S	W

No. - questions name number

N - player name

S - score

w - who won

Scores

No.	N	S	N	S	N	S	N	S	W

No. - questions name number

N - player name

S - score

w - who won

Scores

No.	N	S	N	S	N	S	N	S	W

No. - questions name number

N - player name

S - score

w - who won

Scores

No.	N	S	N	S	N	S	N	S	W

No. - questions name number

N - player name

S - score

w - who won

Scores

No.	N	S	N	S	N	S	N	S	W

No. - questions name number

N - player name

S - score

w - who won

Scores

No.	N	S	N	S	N	S	N	S	W

No. - questions name number

N - player name

S - score

w - who won

Scores

No.	N	S	N	S	N	S	N	S	W

No. - questions name number

N - player name

S - score

w - who won

Printed in Great Britain
by Amazon

70137887R00047